YUNJIN PARK

Dedication

For my parents and grandmother who made it possible for me to write this novel.

Table of Contents

1. On the Tree
2. The Hole
3. How to go Back
4. The War of Bananas
5. The Palace
6. The Great Chess Game
7. King Chessi
8. Super-Duper Hyper Banana Monkey Wonderland
9. 1 vs. a Zillion
10. Escaping
11. Back to Home
12. The Lunch

YUNJIN PARK

Chapter 1: On the Tree

In a small town in Newark, New Jersey, there was an ordinary house with a red roof and large windows. Andy Johnson was eating bananas in a large tree in the beautiful garden at the back of his home. He was watching the cars get stuck in front of the traffic lights. In the garden, there were flowers and insects, including butterflies and bees making pollen.

The bananas, Andy was eating, were so sweet so the bees were coming to him. He was prepared for this; he had brought a jar of honey into the tree with him. Andy opened the honey jar and scooped some out onto a branch beneath him. He did not want to share his bananas with the bees because he was hungry.

One time when he was five years old, a bee came into the kitchen while Andy was opening a jar of honey. He accidentally spilled the entire jar on the carpet and got punished by his mom. That week, he didn't receive any money even when he did all his chores.

Andy didn't think it was fair because it was an accident. His mom was harsh with her punishments so he liked his dad more. His dad always bought him crackers on his way home from the store.

Andy was a young, seven-year-old child that had beautiful blue eyes like the waves of the Pacific Ocean and curly brown hair. He had yellow teeth because he always secretly ate lollipops before bed. His mom didn't know *that* was the reason why they were so yellow, and Andy knew he would be scolded if his mom found out about it. He always wore a red beret because it was his favorite souvenir from Paris. His uncle lives there and sometimes sends Andy and his sister gifts.

Andy's uncle works in the Louvre Museum. He likes to paint pictures at the weekend, when he's off work. He sometimes sends his pictures to Andy's family. Andy's mom proudly displayed them on the walls of their living room. During winter vacations, Andy's sister always went to Paris to attend art classes and she stayed with their uncle.

...

Andy was exhausted from doing his Independence Day chores. He needed to hang a gigantic flag out of the living room window because everyone on his street had a flag. He also needed to finish drawing a flag for homework.

His teacher, Ms. Helen, said they could just draw some of the stars because it was a lot of stars to draw. Over 50! Ms. Helen was the best teacher in the school because she always gave the least amount of homework to her students. However, it didn't matter because he had barely started when his mother saw him grab a piece of paper and told him to draw *all* fifty stars perfectly.

Andy was frustrated because finishing all fifty stars would take one hour. He had heard his friends were doing fun things for Independence Day. His best friends James and Tony were going to a waterpark. They were also having a BBQ together after they got back.

For a rest, Andy went to the tree. He wanted to have a nap under the tree or climb it to watch the cars in traffic. There were too many bees at the base of the tree so he decided to climb the tree, instead of taking a nap. He watched as huge trucks passed by.

'It's amazing' he thought. Andy climbed back down and ran to his room to get his camera. It was the camera he got for his 6th birthday from his grandma. He ran back to check if the last truck was still there but he was too late. The trucks were gone and he could only see normal cars. Andy was frustrated again. He thought this was one of the unluckiest days.

After 30 minutes, his mom gently called, "Andy, time for lunch." Andy thought it could be his favorite food: a hamburger.

"What is it?" Andy curiously asked.

"I'm not telling you!" his mom sang back. He felt annoyed. Ah! Every time she says, "I'm not telling you!" it always meant salad. Why is lunch on

Independence Day so yucky? Andy truly hated salad because he once saw a salad at Christmas on the dinner table and when his mom forced him to eat it, he fiercely threw the bowl away. Because of that, Andy wasn't allowed to eat his dinner that day.

...

Soon, when Andy was trying to climb down the tree, he noticed a big hole at the base. 'Huh. Pretty cool,' Andy thought. Straightaway, Andy thought about two things. 'It would be too dangerous if I fell in. However, breaking all my bones is *a little better* than eating a salad.'

The sudden thought of salads reminded him of how on Christmas, birthdays, on Halloween, and at every exciting holiday, salads were served. This made Andy frustrated. He decided to avoid yet another salad, he would jump into the hole.

He stretched his back, stood up, swung from the branch above, flipped twice and smoothly dove headfirst into the dark hole. Once his hands let go of the branch, he screamed like he was riding the most exciting rollercoaster ever.

Chapter 2: In the Hole

Into the hole, he disappeared. There were sharp rocks on the walls and magical insects that could fly without wings. The walls were beautiful and they looked like they were alive. The rocks in the walls were emitting a soft yellow light.

As Andy looked around, he noticed something else was strange. He was falling in slow motion. It felt like he was lying on a bed. This was a brand-new feeling for him. He didn't know what to do with his arms or legs.

Andy shivered. 'Ah inside this hole is quite cold.' It felt like -1,874 degrees. Andy longed for the black jacket that he bought at the mall last year at Christmas time. After a few minutes, Andy thought, '1km is 100m so I might be 1km down already'. Actually, Andy didn't know what temperature it was or how far he'd fallen because he always thought about the cookies, that he'd seen in the bakery, while he was in class. He was always distracted because he was always looking at Tony's desk which always had a cookie on it.

The bakery was very popular among the kids in his school. It was the place where Andy bought lollipops and sometimes cakes. He wanted to buy cookies but it was too expensive for him to buy. He was saving his money for a blue, Superman bicycle. His friends and Andy always bought cakes there with their parents when it was someone's birthday.

Andy harshly landed on the ground with a huge crash. Luckily, he didn't get hurt because of the magic that was making him float the whole way down. Andy was so tired because he skipped his nap that he lost consciousness for a while. After walking up, Andy was quite dizzy but after a little bit of time, he felt better.

When Andy looked down, he noticed he had landed in a large pile of jewelry. In the pile, there were fancy crowns, shiny coins and colorful necklaces. He dug through and found lots of expensive things. Andy put in his bag a golden cup for his mom, a golden watch for his dad, a golden pen for his sister, a golden candle for his grandma, and a golden canvas for his uncle.

Andy decided to look around the hole. He started to crawl around. He noticed an enormous treasure chest under the pile. However, when he tried to open it, he discovered it was locked.

"Where is the key?" Andy murmured out loud. Andy searched for the key in the pile of jewelry. Instantly, he remembered where he was and cried, "Oh no! I don't know how I'm going to get back up!"

Chapter 3: How to go back

Andy was worried about whether he can see his parents again or not. He tried to jump up like the Superman he saw when he watched a movie at Jamie's house once.

"Oh, I'm going up!"

But it didn't last long and he fell about ten seconds later. It was not Andy's jump that made him feel like it was working, the magic in the hole was causing Andy to float a while in the air. He thought, 'Hmm. If I could make stairs by breaking the walls, I could go up.' Andy tried to kick the wall to give him enough strength to fly upwards but it only made Andy's foot hurt. He also tried to make stairs with coins in art class.

Andy had no hope but pretended to be an optimist because his grandma said he should always be an optimist.

"Firefighters will help me or police officers once my family notices I'm missing. I hope my parents call them." Andy was depressed. His tears were dropping on the jewelry. Slowly Andy's tears fell to the floor and hit a sparkling key.

"Whoa! Maybe it's the key to the treasure chest," Andy said. Andy carefully opened the treasure chess. Surprisingly, a bright light shone and a man looking like a statue of liberty made of wood came out. He had a crown that had 7 points and he was holding a book that had the title "Everything about Chess".

"Are you the Statue of Liberty?" Andy inquired with wide eyes.

"No. My name is the King of Chess, and I was born on thirteenth of February in 1789. I was locked in the chess board because I stole B. M's banana."

"Why are you so tiny?" Andy asked, "and who is B.M.?"

"Because I was in the chess board. I'm not usually this tiny. I could be as gigantic as you."

Suddenly, the king's head became ten times larger and his whole body grew with a loud knock of his foot on the ground.

Chapter 4: The War of Bananas

"Also, you asked who B.M. is. Hmm, B.M. is an evil monkey. Our citizens of the Palace of Chess were killed by the monkeys because they believed bananas were their God. We believed the God is Queen of Chess. She could move the quickest in the palace. We can't see her because she's *that* fast," the King of Chess said proudly.

"Actually, the Palace of Chess and the Super-Duper Hyper Banana Monkey Wonderland have had a war for 3000 years. Our knights were killed by the

'Sphinx' in the door of Super-Duper Hyper Banana Monkey Wonderland."

Andy listened carefully and started to become curious about why the King of Chess was in the chess board.

"Why were you in the board?" Andy curiously asked. "One day, some monkeys came to our palace and grabbed me while singing, 'B.M., B.M. our pharaoh, he said to lock you up! You will go inside this chess board.' I was in the chess board for 500 years but then I heard you and you helped me!"

Andy could imagine the bishops praying to the Queen of Chess to win the war. The King of Chess continued, "the war has lasted for 3,000 years. Five kings tried to win the war."

"First, King Cheliam tried but he was too fat so he easily got shot. Second, King Chedward had a banana allergy and failed when the monkeys threw bananas into his mouth. Third, King Chames had a foolish horse and it slipped on the banana peels and flew away onto a banana tree. His skeleton is still up in the tree. The fourth King was Chessi and he accidentally ate a poisoned potato and died. My dad Chelly needed to be the king but he disappeared mysteriously when he was a prince, so I am the fifth king. However, none before me have succeeded. We will win because our civilization is better. B.M.'s civilization is still at the same level as when the species in the hole started making civilizations."

Andy admired the King of Chess's confidence but he didn't believe all of what the King of Chess said because it sounded too unbelievable.

"Will you come to my palace?"

"How?" Andy questioned.

"Using this door!" The door was so tiny only a rat can fit through it. "I'm not a rat!" Andy shouted. Because of his nickname 'rat', he felt angered. IT just meant he's short. Andy's sister was the first to call him 'rat', but Jane had overheard and she kept calling him rat. Jane was the worst bully in Andy's grade.

Andy didn't care about her but lots of his friends got frustrated by Jane.

Once, Jane stole Duke's soccer ball and threw it onto the road. Duke was frustrated because Duke really loved soccer.

The King of Chess saw Andy get distracted by these thoughts so he pretended to do a ridiculous, fake sneeze. Andy whipped his head around to look at him. The King of Chess continued with a small grin on his face, "the door being small won't be a problem." Instantly, the door became larger with a small tap of his crown. Andy gasped because he'd never seen magic even in magic shows.

"Let's go!" Andy thought it would be fun because he thought King of Chess was a funny person.

Chapter 5: The Palace

Inside the door, there was a new world. Andy saw a wonderful waterfall made of rainbow juice. The juice was of a mixture of lots of flavors like orange, apple, cranberry and more. "Wow! It's amazing!" Andy gasped. "Nope. We have more beautiful things in the palace," the King of Chess bragged. Andy was excited to tour the palace. He wanted to see more interesting things.

Suddenly, a flying carpet came to the King of Chess. Andy declared, "Wow is this what you are talking about?" "No," the King of Chess answered.

Andy rode the flying carpet on his stomach like Superman from the movie he saw at Jamie's house. The carpet flew up to the sky, and over the clouds and finally, the King of Chess and Andy saw the palace. "Is this it?" Andy quizzed. "No," the King of Chess stated harshly.

The carpet flew quickly through the clouds and the palace came into view. The palace looked like a castle from the Middle Ages; very old and made of gray bricks. They flew through a door and they were finally inside the palace. All the surfaces were covered with chess boards made from gold and silver. Knights and bishops were walking around the palace, it looked like some were praying and some were searching for monkey spies. "This definitely should be the thing. Isn't it?" Andy asked hopefully.

The King of Chess was silent. Andy thought the King of Chess was acting strange because he always spoke to him even if it was just to say 'no'. The knights fiercely grabbed Andy by his arms and started to pull him away. Andy screamed but the knights didn't care. The jail was in the dungeon. The knights put a towel over Andy's head to not allow him to see where he was going. However, Andy could smell some dead creatures. The knights threw him through the doors of a cell and the King of Chess shouted, "This is the beautiful jail that you will wait in until I eat some food, you little kid!"

Andy thought he got betrayed because the King of Chess had him removed from the main palace. A minute later, the knights took off the towel. He saw other prisoners; they were all young children, like Andy. They had also been caught like Andy.

Chapter 6: The Great Chess Game

Andy was lying on the floor, imagining what will happen to him next. 'Maybe I will be killed by the knights. Or maybe I will be in this jail forever,' Andy wondered.

"Wow! That was a good lunch. I'm thankful that time doesn't exist so I could eat 24,601 lunches in a day," someone announced.

Andy heard the King of Chess coming. He knew it was him because he recognized the King of

Chess's voice. His footsteps were like a T-Rex, like the one Andy saw in a movie in a movie theatre. He tried to hide in the darkest part of the cell because he was scared.

"Turn on the lights!"

The lights turned on, and Andy was caught by the King of Chess.

"Let's make a deal, kid," the King of Chess muttered. "If I win against you in a game of chess, you get the jewelry from B.M. for me. And if you win, I will tell you where the ladder is."

Andy was confused about what to do. He didn't believe what the King of Chess was saying. After all, he was the reason Andy had been put in jail.

He knew that it was the only way to get a chance to climb up the hole. "Okay," Andy agreed. Andy thought it would be a hard game of chess against the King of Chess.

Andy followed the King of Chess. The lights suddenly flickered off. "Monkeys, I bet they cut the electricity lines again!" the King of Chess complained. Andy couldn't see anything but he felt the bodies of dead rats under his shoes. Andy bet the jail had a cat in it which could explain all of the dead rats. Andy and the King of Chess went into the next room of the dungeon.

Once they were sitting, the game began. Andy was so nervous that his hands were trembling.

The King of Chess looked very confident though. During the game, the King of Chess only moved the king because he was a king. Andy was perplexed and used the knights to kill the King of Chess's king. Andy easily beat the King of Chess. He felt like flying. He was so excited that he danced every dance move that he knew.

Suddenly, the hand of the King of Chess vanished. From his finger to his wrist, it was gone. Andy was very surprised. "This is our King's curse," the King said softly, "We lose our body parts when we lose a game of chess." Andy couldn't help but feel cheerless for the King of Chess. There was a moment of silence, then he spoke, "Come on. Let's go get the ladder."

On the way through the hallways, Andy saw many pictures. Under one picture of monkeys getting caught by the knights, "The Wonderful Jewelry Defense War," was written. In another picture, there were knights stealing bananas. It had "July, Banana Stealing War," written beside it. Andy read out loud, "King Chessi without his head, fight for Super-Duper Hyper Banana Monkey Wonderland War IV." Andy thought, 'Maybe he lost a chess game and lost his head.'

Andy kept walking. "Now, here is the portal that we will use." On either side of the portal, there were sculptures of the kings that had been at war with the monkeys. "Let's go," the King of Chess muttered. The portal made Andy feel like his soul was leaving his body.

In the portal, Andy passed a lot of rooms, Mouse Room, Cheddar Cheese Room, Bee Room. Without warning, thousands of elephants stormed out of Elephant Room. "What is this?" Andy loudly asked. "Ah. They're just going to the water room to drink some water," explained the King of Chess. Andy had never seen so many elephants before.

After a few minutes, they arrived at the Super-Duper Hyper Banana Monkey Wonderland. The King of Chess wrote the password 'banana' on the keypad. "This is the password that our previous king, King Chessi, made. He was the best king of our palace. The monkeys don't know our password so they can't use the portal."

Chapter 7: King Chessi

The King of Chess was excited to tell Andy all about King Chessi. "King Chessi once pretended to be a monkey by wearing a costume and went into the Super-Duper Hyper Banana Monkey Wonderland riding a boat through the Banile river, which is the longest river in the hole. He noticed that the monkeys only know how to write the word 'banana'.

He went into a pyramid and saw ancient pictures and wall etchings using only the word 'banana'. He came back and made the password:

chess. When he writes 'chess', the door opens. When the monkeys try to write 'banana', a bell rings and the knights shoot arrows at the monkeys. When King Chessi ruled, 1,782,567 monkeys wrote banana and were shot. He also knows the Sphinx's password too.

One time, a gigantic monkey sculpture was being built and a Sphinx asked. 'What is the password?' The monkey that was driving the boat said 'Banana.' The monkey looked like an old slave."

Andy actually didn't know what a slave was but he just thought it was like a king. "How do you know all that?" Andy inquired.

"It's because I heard about it when I was 50 years old. I was in first grade and my grandpa, King

Chessi told me during a chess game! That's when he lost concentration and lost against me. He lost his head and went back to fight in the next war. He said it was useful because he'd never be shot in his head by an arrow."

"Then how could he fight without seeing?" Andy asked. "In our king DNA, we feel a new feeling when we lose a feeling. He always used that new feeling and his sword to help him get to the correct place." Andy thought it's a cool thing.

After hearing the entire story, Andy didn't want to go to Super-Duper Hyper Banana Monkey Wonderland. He could only think about all the terrible monkeys are living there.

Andy slowly went towards the door for Super-Duper Hyper Banana Monkey Wonderland. "Bye," the King of Chess whispered. "I have to leave now or else the monkeys will kill me." Andy was just about to ask why, when the King of Chess magically disappeared and left Andy alone. Andy took a deep breath and jumped through the door.

Chapter 8: Super-Duper Hyper Banana Monkey Wonderland

....

Andy entered the Super-Duper Hyper Banana Monkey Wonderland and saw a tall mountain and an amazing palace made of bananas. He wondered if the palace would be yummy. He also noticed monkeys singing and going up to the mountain. Andy thought there could be around 300 to 400 monkeys going up the mountain.

"B.M., B.M., our boss, he likes bananas so he's Banana Monkey. We are going to find bananas because we don't know how to get seeds," chanted a group of monkeys not so far away from Andy.

Andy turned around and noticed that there were zillions of monkeys were protecting a ladder. The ladder was important for the monkeys to protect because it was the only way to go out of the hole. Andy felt depressed and looked up. He noticed B.M. eyeballing him. Once their eyes met, Andy knew he was in trouble.

B.M. shouted, "Banana stealing machine, steal those bananas!" Andy had forgotten that he'd stuffed his extra bananas in his bag before jumping into the hole. "Ee-oh!" The machine made a noise. B.M. sighed and made a face. Andy realized that the machine was broken. "Ah! My monkeys, steal the bananas NOW!!" B.M. roared like thunder.

In a split second, zillions of monkeys jumped towards Andy and his bag. Andy had a hard time breathing because of the monkeys that were on top of him. 'I need to get rid of this banana bag.' Andy quickly threw the bag to his right with all his strength. The bag rolled into the portal. All the monkeys jumped into the portal. The door was still open. Andy heard the monkeys fighting each other over the bag.

Andy didn't have any energy to move for a few seconds but once he caught his breath, he jumped to his feet and lunged to grab a hold of the ladder. The once loud monkeys were now quiet. Andy thought it was strange. He looked behind him and saw that every single monkey was coldly staring at him.

Chapter 9: 1 vs. a Zillion

....

The monkeys fiercely commanded in unison, "Give us back the ladder." Andy pretended he was giving them the ladder but quickly hit a monkey on his head. The monkey flew quite far. Andy was surprised by how far it went.

Other monkeys with frustrated faces came towards him but they were also hit by the ladder. The fight lasted one minute but Andy felt like it had been an hour. The monkeys that had been hit had started to fall on top of each other and they made a gigantic pile on a banana tree.

"Oh! Oh!" a noise came out from the Banana Palace. Andy noticed B.M. was coming to try to fight him. He was sliding like a figure-skater on banana peels. No matter how much he tried to move towards Andy, he kept sliding to the opposite side of the door. There were too many banana peels on the floor, so he slipped with each step.

"Oh! Oh! Ah! Ah!" B.M. cried out.

"What is he saying?" Andy asked himself.

"It means that he's angry," a baby monkey cutely answered from a tree nearby.

"Thanks!" Andy said, surprised by how nice this baby monkey was being to him.

He thought this monkey was definitely better than the King of Chess. Andy slid down a rock like a slide and stopped in front of the portal. B.M. was still screaming and struggling to gain any ground to move toward Andy. By this time, Andy was already in the portal.

Chapter 10: Escaping

....

Andy rushed into the portal. Once he closed the door, he started to move through the hallway. He saw many rooms on the way back too. He saw foxes coming out of the fox room and going into the hen room. Maybe they're hungry and are going to eat some hens.'

Andy went in front of the door that had Chess Palace written on it. Andy thought, 'the password will perhaps be 'B.M. is dumb''. Andy wrote 'B.M. is dumb'. He thought that King of Chess hates B.M. the most so surely that's what the password would be. However, the keypad turned red, and Andy knew that meant the password was wrong. "Or could it be 'chess', like the other ones," Andy wondered. He pressed the buttons to spell out 'chess' and the door opened. Andy went into the Chess Palace. Once inside he placed the ladder against the wall beside the door.

"I was waiting for you, young kid!" the King of Chess said from in front of the portal. "Knights! Catch him!" The knights jumped towards Andy. Andy jumped up and stepped over them by scaling up on top of the pictures on the wall. The knights tried to grab Andy's shoulders but they foolishly crashed into each other.

"No! My grandpa's picture!" The King of Chess had a depressed look on his face as all his pictures crashed to the floor. Andy jumped to the light fixtures next.

"My money! My money!" the King of Chess screamed. He screamed louder when each crystal fell.

Andy finally reached the door to go out of the palace. He jumped on to the ground and started to run as fast as he could, after grabbing the ladder from where he'd left it. He thought his legs were going to fall off because of how fast he was moving. He reached the bottom of the hole after three minutes. He quickly placed the ladder against the wall of the hole and started to rapidly climb up the ladder.

He felt heavier than before because there were a bunch of coins, from the pile of jewelry, in his pockets. He would use them to buy a new bicycle. When Andy was almost to the top of the hole, he felt the ladder start to shake like an earthquake. Andy looked down and saw the King of Chess had grabbed the ladder and was trying to throw the ladder away. Andy jumped using all his strength to catch the edge of the hole and finally he reached up to grab the ground.

The King of Chess and his knights tried to shoot arrows at Andy's body but Andy dodged them.

Andy rolled out of the hole to under the tree. He felt the warm sun on his skin and breathed in the clean air. Andy noticed he was back under the tree. His heart was racing but soon it started to calm down.

Chapter 11: Back to Home

....

"Whoa! I need to rest!" Andy lay on the grass. 'Our garden's grass is the best.' A butterfly landed on his hand. "I like butterflies. They always come to me." Andy rested for several minutes.

"Hmm. I think I need to check the hole. If the King of Chess uses the ladder to chase me, I might still be in danger."

Andy slowly stood up and took a few steps over to where the hole had been. However, the hole was gone. "I should dig it back," he muttered to himself. He started to dig but nothing related to the hole came out of the soil. One penny... a cola can... soil and a few worms. His bag was gone forever and so were the gifts he had collected for his family. He felt like it was a dream. Then, a coin fell out of his pocket. Andy was excited because he knew this meant where he'd been and what he'd seen had been real. He was excited and relieved.

He dug his hand into his pocket and found more coins, as he counted them, he thought he had enough to buy a bicycle. He would have to hide the bicycle because his mom wouldn't believe his story and might punish him. She might think that he stole the money from someone at night.

Chapter 12: The Lunch

....

"Andy, I waited for you for ten minutes to eat lunch," his mom shouted from the back door of his house. "Okay mom. Coming!" 'Was I really only gone for ten minutes?' Andy asked himself. Andy was curious and went to the dining room.

He saw his favorite plate and his favorite soda already in his glass. The tables looked cleaner than normal. Also, in the center, was his sister's favorite flower, a rose, in a vase. Andy scanned the table for the infamous salad he knew he'd have to eat. However, he didn't see one. Instead, he saw hamburgers! Andy was so surprised that he couldn't say anything.

"I actually wanted to eat a salad," his sister quietly muttered. Andy made a yucky face to his sister. 'It's going to be so yummy!' Andy devoured his hamburger quickly. The burger tasted as good as flying on the magic carpet felt. He had another one after.

Later that evening, while he was lying in bed with his belly full of hamburgers, he thought about the jail in the Chess Palace and the monkeys piling on top of him. He was relieved to be safe and sound at home and understood not everything turns out how you expect it to. Like the King of Chess losing his hand, and how B.M. kept slipping on the banana peels. Or how there was no salad on the dining table for lunch.

Finally, as he closed his heavy eyes, he felt grateful to be home, grateful to have gone on an adventure, and grateful to have learned how to play chess. That night in his dream, his mom was B.M. and his dad was the King of Chess.

YUNJIN PARK

About the Author

Yunjin Park was born in 2014 in Seoul, South Korea. He is in the 5th grade in Seoul Namsung Elementary School. His dream is to become an architect and design a landmark in Seoul.

During in his free time, he plays many kinds of sports but his favorite is baseball. He also enjoys playing video games and spending time with his friends. He is interested in the history of many countries around the world.

Yunjin is inspired by the author Roald Dahl because the books that he writes always makes the readers laugh. He enjoys fantasy novels.

Under the Hole is Yunjin's first novel.

발 행 일	2024년 11월 15일
저 자	YUNJIN PARK
감 수	TRACEY GILLIAN
표지디자인	YUNJIN PARK
발 행 인	윤미경
발 행 처	(주)이스피릿
등 록	제 2016-000086호
I S B N	979-11-92868-65-3
주 소	서울시 서초구 서초대로 42길 69